SEP – – 2009

SLEEPING DRAGONS ALL AROUND

Sheree Fitch

Illustrations by
Michele Nidenoff

NIMBUS
PUBLISHING

Nimbus Publishing Limited
PO Box 9166
Halifax, NS   B3K 5M8
(902) 455-4286   www.nimbus.ca

Printed and bound in Canada

Design: Co. & Co. Design
Author photo: Gilles Plante
Illustrator photo: IPC Canada Photo Services Inc.

Library and Archives Canada Cataloguing in Publication

Fitch, Sheree
Sleeping dragons all around / Sheree Fitch, author ;
Michele Nidenoff, illustrator. — 20th anniversary ed.
ISBN 978-1-55109-699-5

I. Nidenoff, Michele II. Title.
PS8561.I86S5 2009   jC813'.54   C2008-906626-X

We acknowledge the financial support of the Government of Canada
through the Book Publishing Industry Development Program (BPIDP) and
the Canada Council, and of the Province of Nova Scotia through the Depart-
ment of Tourism, Culture and Heritage for our publishing activities.

—

A NOTE ON THE NEW EDITION

How can a book be a book if it doesn't get read, or a poem be a poem if it doesn't get said? The answer is that it takes readers and listeners to bring a book to life. This storyteller is grateful that *Sleeping Dragons All Around* found a home in so many lives and is now being read to a second generation. May you always share your cake and share this book and dance with dragons in the world of words.

She hurried at his words, beset with fears

For there were sleeping dragons all around

At glaring watch, perhaps with ready spears,

Down the wide stairs, a darkling way they found—

In all the house was heard no human sound.

— from **THE EVE OF ST. AGNES**

John Keats

Over there on a quilt
Of saffron and silk
Lies Priscilla
In pink pantaloons
Priscilla prefers
Marabou furs
Her earrings are blue balloons
Priscilla's the queen
Of the movie star scene
Asleep she appears most gentle
But I've heard it said
That when not in bed
She's extremely temperamental

So I must tiptoe...
Tiptoe...
Softly
As I pass...

Fagan the Dragon's
A hideous sight
His scales are gold, they glitter at night
He has spiked his hair and dyed it green
He shrank his shirt
In the washing machine
What is most bizarre
Is the silver star
That Fagan wears through his nose
Fagan smells like onions
And sleeps here when it snows

And so...
Plug my nose...
Here it goes...

I must tiptoe
Tiptoe...
Softly
As I pass...

In our tub sleeps Beelzebub
Surrounded by suds and soap
With a snorkel on her snout
She breathes through a periscope
Beelzebub blows blue bubbles
As she dreams away her troubles
Sometimes she leaves puddles
On the bathroom floor.

(If Beelzebub got out of her tub,
I'd get wet
I bet.)

So I must tiptoe
Tiptoe...
Softly
As I pass...

Glump
Is simply
A dimplish
Blimpish
Balloon belly
A slumpish lump
A WIMP of a dragon
With his tail
Zigzaggin around the room
His chin
Draggin along the floor
With HICCUPS
Like no one's heard before
The whole floor shakes
But Glump NEVER wakes

(I hope)

So I must tiptoe
Tiptoe...
Softly
As I pass...

Over there by the stair
Sleeps the dragon Pythagorus
A dragon of deadly precision
His obsession is mathematics
He's unusually adept at division
The dragon Pythagorus
Counts in his sleep
I strongly suspect
That he tabulates sheep,
The dragon Pythagorus
Drutters away
Until night has melted into day:

"Numbers! Numbers!
Infinitesimal!
I love numbers
Especially decimals!"

And so...
With a 1 and a 2 and a 3
I must tiptoe
Tiptoe...
Softly
As I pass...

Ching-Chung hangs
Upside down
In his
Majestical
Ancestral
Pure silk gown
Crimson
Amethyst
Silver and gold
He's one thousand
    And two
        And a half
           Years old.

Ching-Chung sings
Of dragonish things
"Where is the butter
In a butterfly's wings?"
Ching-Chung snores
Through his ancient nose
The fire he breathes
Might burn my toes
(I wish I'd brought the garden hose)

        So I tiptoe
          FAST
            PAST
              Ching-Chung

There in his lair
In a rocking chair
Sleeps old Jebediah Jones
His skin sags like garbage bags
Brittle are his bones

Jebediah has three long whiskers
Sprouting from his snout
Occasionally he uses tweezers
And tries to pluck them out
He smells a bit like medicine
That's gone a little stale
He daily swallows vitamins
And drinks golden gingerale.
Even though his stomach droops
As if he's wrapped in hula-hoops
One can always hear him hum
Some ancient dragon hymn
Each and every night
When Jebediah
Comes in

So I must tiptoe
Tiptoe....
Softly
As I pass...

Stretched out flat
On my trampoline
Is that muscular dragon
Ms. Lindy Lean
She teaches aerobics
At the Y.D.C.A.
She works out with weights
At least four times a day
Her sneakers are GARGANTUAN
So is her jogging suit
She maintains a health food diet
Of salad and yogurt and fruit
Ms. Lindy Lean
Is incredibly keen
Her muscles are mountains it seems
I think she's even doing
Push-ups in her dreams.

So I must tiptoe
Tiptoe...
Softly
As I pass...

Shhhh! SHHH!
I'm just about there
Even with dragons everywhere

OH NOOOOOO!
I STUBBED MY TOE!

I said "OOOOOOOOOWWWWWWWWWW!

And now
The sleeping dragons are AWAKE

Thundering, blundering
Closer and closer...

Oh NOOOOOO!

They're growling and grumbling
They're crunchin' and munchin'

MY MOCHA MAPLE CHOCOLATE CAKE

"YOU BOLD AND BRUTISH BURSTEN-BELLIED BEASTS...
YOU...YOU BRASH BUNCH OF BEDRAGGLED DRAGONS...
YOU...YOU GOBBLERS
YOU...YOU THIEVES
YOU—"

I place my finger on each snout
Command them with
My loudest shout—

I blink:
They shrink
Then slink
Away...

"DRAGONS DREAD
GO BACK TO BED !! "

Tiptoe...
      Tiptoe...
            Off *they* go
With their heads hanging low
Dragon teardrops in their eyes

And so...

I yell
"Surprise, surprise!
Since you dragons are awake
I'll give you each one piece
Of my Mocha
      Maple
      Chocolate
      Cake."

The cake is deeee-light-ful
Dee-dragon-dee-licious!
We dance in the kitchen
We don't do the dishes.

Then we all
    Tiptoe...
        Tiptoe...
           Softly
              Back to bed.